Illustrated
by
Tony Benford

Copyright

Note from the author

Dear Reader,

If you have ever suddenly and spontaneously started dancing because something made you happy, then this book is for you! These moments can happen after some good food, news of an amazing gift, hearing your favorite song in your head, healing in church or for no reason at all! Happy dances happen all the time, everywhere, they're even going on right this second. They happen on the inside of you where nobody sees or in the middle of a crowd for everyone to witness. A happy dance is for all ages! I want to encourage you to make your own music and dance to the beat of your own drum. But whatever dance you do, do it happy!

With love and kindness,

Tony Benford

I got the power to do

4

I got the power to say

I got the power to do

I got the power
to say

7

When I speak to
this mountain

It moves out my way

When I speak to this mountain

It moves out my way

I've got a mind to think

I've got a mind to learn

I've got a mind to think

I've got a mind to learn

I work hard
everyday

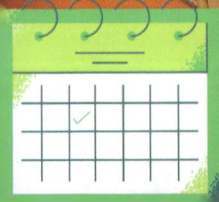

16

I work hard
everyday

I don't care what you heard

March
19

I got a heart to love

I got a heart to feel

I got a heart to love

I got a heart to feel

I believe with the best

I'm just keeping it real

I believe with the best

I'm just keeping it real

27

I got joy in my feet

I got joy in my hands

I got joy in my feet

I got joy in my hands

You just stand there and watch

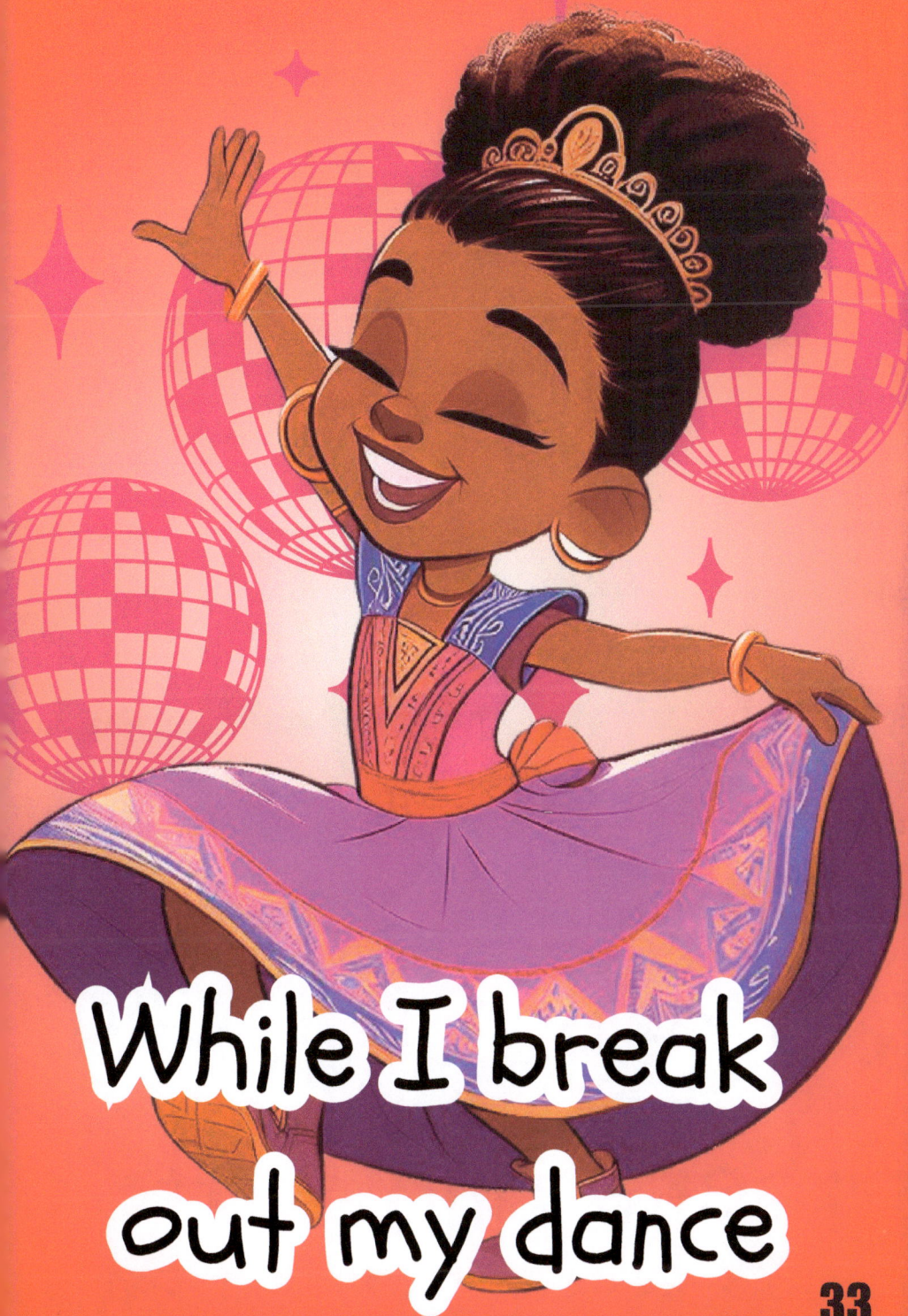

While I break out my dance

You just stand there and watch

While I break out my dance

36

Come on

Everybody do ya

HAPPY DANCE

Everybody do ya

HAPPY DANCE

Everybody do ya

HAPPY DANCE

Everybody do ya

HAPPY DANCE

www.ingramcontent.com/pod-product-compliance
Lightning Source LLC
Chambersburg PA
CBHW041801040426
42447CB00005B/282